Pasch to Pentecost

veritas

Vincent Ryan

Pasch to Pentecost

The Liturgy of Paschaltide

Veritas Publications Dublin 1977

First published 1977 by
Veritas Publications
Pranstown House, Booterstown Avenue, Co. Dublin.

Set in 11/12 Baskerville and
printed and bound in the Republic of Ireland by
Cahill (1976) Limited, Dublin.
Designed by Liam Miller.
Cover by Steven Hope.

Nihil OBSTAT:
Daniel McCarthy

Imprimi POTEST:
+ Dermot,
Archbishop of Dublin.
March 14th 1977

ISBN 0-905092-32-5
Cat. No. 3352

Contents

1 THE MEANING OF PASCHALTIDE

Easter is the oldest and the greatest of the Christian feasts, surpassing even the Nativity in importance. Its celebration in the Easter Vigil constitutes the heart of the liturgical year. This celebration, prepared for by the forty days of Lent, is extended throughout the whole period of fifty days which we call Paschaltide or Easter Time. This is the great season of rejoicing culminating in the feast of Pentecost which completes our Easter celebrations, just as the first Pentecost was the culmination and completion of Christ's redeeming work.

A key to the understanding of this season is provided by the General Roman Calendar in its section on the Easter season:[1]

> The fifty days between Easter Sunday and Pentecost are celebrated as one feastday, sometimes called "the great Sunday". The singing of the alleluia is characteristic of these days. The Sundays of this season are counted as Sundays of Easter.

This is succinct and significant. It shows that the Church today understands Easter and its aftermath in exactly the same way as did the Church of

antiquity. In its vision of Paschaltide the new
Roman Calendar is even more traditional than the
one it has replaced. Let us explain how this is so.

Prior to the reform of the Calendar and Missal,
Paschaltide was presented as an appendage to
Easter rather than as an intrinsic part of Easter
itself and its continuation throughout the fifty-
day period. The Sundays which followed were
called Sundays *after* Easter rather than Sundays
of Easter as is now the case. The season has indeed
a festive and joyful character, but one would not
have described it as an uninterrupted celebration
of Easter itself.

This period belongs to the oldest part of the liturgical year which, in its most primitive form
(3rd century), consisted simply of Sunday, the
Easter Triduum and the fifty days following Easter
Sunday. This period was known as Pentecost or
sometimes as "holy Pentecost". The name did not
originally denote a particular day, the last day of
this season, but the whole season itself.

Pentecost was one long and joyful celebration of
the paschal feast. The whole period had the character of a Sunday, and for the early Church Sunday
was simply a weekly Easter. The fifty days were
viewed as a single day and were even designated as
"the great Sunday" (*magna dominica*). Each day
had the character of a Sunday: fasting was excluded,
kneeling was forbidden — the faithful prayed
standing as a sign of the resurrection, the alleluia
was repeatedly sung as at Easter.

Somehow we must recapture the spirit of the ancient Pentecost and the sense of celebration which was not content with a single day or even an octave to celebrate Easter, but required a whole season. We should see it as a unified whole stretching from Easter Sunday to the evening of the fiftieth day: a period which St Athanasius describes as "the most joyful period" (*laetissimum spatium*).

Celebrating the Resurrection

The mystery of the Resurrection permeates the whole season. This mystery is viewed in all its aspects throughout the fifty days. This is the good news of salvation, the cause of the Church's rejoicing.

The Resurrection is presented both as an historical event and as an ever-present reality, a saving mystery ever at work in the Church. This becomes clear from a study of the paschal liturgy. Beginning with Easter Sunday and its octave we notice that the daily gospels recount the various manifestations of the Risen Lord to his disciples: to Mary Magdalene and the other women, to the two disciples on the road to Emmaus, to the eleven apostles at table, at the lake of Tiberias, to all the apostles including Thomas. These visible manifestations of the Lord, as recorded by the four evangelists, may be regarded as the major theme of the liturgy of the word. This is certainly true of the octave when each day the Easter event is presented to us in a new light.

After the octave the Resurrection is not lost sight of but is viewed from a different perspective. Now it is the active presence in the Church of the risen and glorified Christ which is foremost. He is contemplated as the Good Shepherd who from heaven pastures his sheep, or as the Way leading to the Father, or again as the source of the Spirit and the giver of the living Bread, the Vine from which we the branches derive life and sustenance.

Considered then as an historical event and as a mystery which affects our lives here and now, the Resurrection is the focus of the whole paschal liturgy. This is the season of the Resurrection and so of new life and of hope.

And since this mystery is indeed Good News for the world, it must be witnessed to and proclaimed. The gospels present us with the apostolic witness and require of us the response of faith. There are also the other New Testament writings such as The Acts of the Apostles which record for us the witness borne by the disciples to "the resurrection of the Lord Jesus".

Our sharing in the Resurrection

During this time of Easter we celebrate not only the resurrection of Christ the Head but also that of his members who share in this mystery. That is why baptism figures so prominently in the liturgy.

Through faith and baptism we are drawn into the paschal mystery of the passion, death and resurrection of the Lord. St Paul's exhortation, read out for us at the Easter Vigil, re-echoes through the season:

> You have been taught that when we were baptised in Christ Jesus we were baptised in his death; in other words, when we were baptised we went into the tomb with him and joined him in death, so that as Christ was raised from the dead by the Father's glory, we too might live a new life *(Rom 6: 3-11)*.

It is not enough to recall the mystery, we must show it forth in our lives as well. Risen with Christ, our lives should manifest what we have become. We must "look for the things that are in heaven, where Christ is, sitting at God's right hand" *(Col.3:1)*. This is to share in the freedom of God's sons: to be dead to sin but alive for God in Christ Jesus.

The whole redemptive mystery

The liturgical commemoration of the Resurrection forms the essence of Paschaltide. That does not, however, exhaust the full content of this season. The glorious mysteries of Ascension and Pentecost also belong to this time. Without them the celebration of the paschal mystery would be incomplete.

Now it seems that in very early times, before the liturgical year began to take shape in the fourth century, the Ascension and Pentecost were not celebrated as distinct feasts. They were present, however, in the Church's understanding of Paschaltide. They were commemorated implicitly in the fifty-day cycle and were treated as integral parts of the paschal solemnity. Thus it is not surprising to learn that the whole period could be referred to as "the solemnity of the Spirit". It was as much a continuous Pentecost as a continuous Easter.

Fr Robert Cabié, in an exhaustive study of Pentecost in the first centuries, observes that the early Church in its celebration of what we call Paschaltide commemorated the whole redemptive mystery. This included the Resurrection, the manifestations of the Risen Lord, his ascension into heaven, the descent of the Holy Spirit, the presence of Christ in his Church and the expectation of his glorious return.[2]

In the light of what we know of early Christianity the pentecostal period celebrated the Christian mystery in its totality, just as Sunday, the Lord's day, celebrated the whole paschal mystery. Both the weekly Sunday and the "great Sunday" introduced the whole Body of Christ into the glory acquired by the Head.

The experience of the early Church can enrich our own understanding of Paschaltide. An important part of that experience was a keen awareness of the presence of Christ in his Church. This presence continues to be highlighted in the liturgy and is symbolised by the paschal candle in the church sanctuary. In The Acts of the Apostles the forty days between Easter and Ascension are recorded as a time when the Risen Lord is visibly present to his Church; he even eats and drinks with his disciples. The Church today, as in the past, celebrates this historical presence and at the same time celebrates Christ's presence here and now, a presence actualised in the liturgical mystery. In this paschal season, the Church, the Bride of Christ, rejoices to be re-united with the Bridegroom (see *Lk 5:34-35*).

2 The joy of Paschaltide

No other liturgical season is so characterised by joy. Everything in the liturgy — the music and song, the vestments, the readings and other texts — give expression to this. This joy and exuberance is summed up in the cry of Alleluia which is heard repeatedly throughout the season. On Easter night this acclamation was intoned three times by the priest or deacon and repeated by the people; it heralded the Good News of the Resurrection. It had been suppressed during the long penitential season, and now it breaks forth once more as the Easter eucharist is about to be celebrated.

Alleluia is a Hebrew word which simply means "Praise God". It is an acclamation which the Church has inherited from the Old Testament and so is a link with the worship of the Temple and synagogue. Its meaning cannot be conveyed by a traslation since it is expressive of religious feeling rather than of thought; it evokes a whole atmosphere of praise and rejoicing. Ideally it will be sung.

People today are unlikely to become excited about the Easter alleluia, as was the case in the past and is still the case with Christians of the Eastern tradition. (For spontaneous joy one needs to assist at an Easter celebration in an Eastern-rite church.) Still, the renewed liturgy has led us to a better appreciation of such acclamations as the alleluia; and where this is sung, it does indeed express the joy of a congregation.

What is certain is that alleluia is one of the key-words of the Easter liturgy and perfectly expresses the deep-felt joy of this time. It is not surprising then that the Church fathers not only referred to the alleluia in their preaching but loved to expound it in their Easter homilies. This is very characteristic of St Augustine who returned to this theme again and again in his paschal instructions. Here is one example:

> The alleluia is said throughout these fifty days. For alleluia indicates praise of God; hence, to us who are labouring it signifies the attainment of our rest. For when we come to that rest after this period of labour, our sole occupation will be the praise of God, our action there will be Alleluia . . . there alleluia will be our food, alleluia will be our drink, alleluia will be our peaceful action, alleluia will be our whole joy.[1]

In the office of readings for Paschaltide we find two further examples of this type of catechesis. One is entitled "Let us sing to the Lord a song of love" and the other "The Paschal Alleluia".[2] We

can only refer to them here, but they deserve
attentive reading.

A foretaste of eternal joy

St Augustine sees the alleluia as an anticipation of
the heavenly liturgy. He sounds an eschatological
note. This is typical of the fathers and it introduces
us to an important aspect of Easter joy. The joy of
Paschaltide is an anticipation of the joy of God's
kingdom. This is a constant theme with Augustine
who observes: "These holy days which are celebrated after the resurrection of the Lord signify the
life that is to come after our resurrection".[3] St
Athanasius, in his *Festal Letters*, also develops this
thought:

> When the first day of the holy week dawns
> and rises upon us let us keep feast on the holy
> day of Pentecost. Let us keep feast on the
> first day of the great week as a symbol of the
> world to come, in which we here receive a
> pledge that we shall have everlasting life here-
> after. Then, having passed from hence we
> shall keep a perfect feast with Christ.[4]

This Easter joy then is a sign and foretaste of
future happiness and fulfilment. It is not yet the
full reality but merely the promise and the first in-
stalment of "what eye has not seen nor ear heard".
    The interior source of this joy is the Holy Spirit.
Where there is true joy there the Holy Spirit is at

work. We read for example in Acts that "the disciples were filled with joy and the Holy Spirit" (*13:52*). It is as though the one were a necessary concomitant of the other.

And if Easter joy is a foretaste, a pointer to what lies ahead, so is our possession of the Holy Spirit. We have truly received him, he has entered our lives. His presence is a promise of the blessings which are destined for us. St Paul likes to describe this presence of the Holy Spirit as a pledge or guarantee. He is "the guarantee of our inheritance until we acquire possession of it" (*Eph 1:14*). The apostle also refers to him as the first fruits: "We have received the first fruits of the Spirit" (*Rom 8:23*).

Already we possess eternal life, at least in a partial or initial way. This is cause for rejoicing even if our joy is limited in various ways by our own human condition, our trials, interior and exterior, and our constant struggle against sin. This leads us to speak of the Cross.

The commemoration of the Cross

When Jesus appeared to his disciples on the evening of the first Easter Sunday, he "showed them his hands and his side" (*Jn 20:20*). He showed them his wounds, preserved in his glorified body. The Passion and the Cross are not forgotten after the Resurrection.

Nor does the Church blot out the memory of

Calvary during Paschaltide. The Cross is also commemorated in the liturgy. In the office of readings we have some fine patristic homilies on the Cross and Passion. On Friday of the second week of Easter (*Divine Office 11*, p. 522), St Theodore the Studite addresses us:

> It (the Cross) is the tree on which the Lord, like a great warrior with his hands and feet and his divine side pierced in battle, healed the wounds of our sins, healed our nature that had been wounded by the evil serpent.

The Cross is not lost sight of in Paschaltide. Transfigured, it is true, in the light of Easter glory, it is none the less there. It is commemorated especially on the Fridays of Easter but there are allusions to it on other days as well. In passing we refer the reader to two other Passion sermons in the Breviary. One of them is by St Ephraem on "Christ's Cross and the salvation of the human race" and is given on Friday of the third week (*Divine Office 11*, p. 546); the other is by St Cyril and is headed "Christ gave his body for the life of all" (*Saturday of third week, ibid.* p. 550). The aim of these fathers is not primarily to arouse sentiments of compassion and repentance but rather to strengthen our faith in the life-giving power of the Cross.

The Cross is not absent from the celebration of Easter; nor is it ever absent from our own lives. There is no closed season to suffering, nor any time when we are not exhorted to carry our cross. This need not trouble us, however. Not only can joy co-exist with suffering, it also has a secret affinity with it. This may appear a strange paradox, and so it is. The lives of the saints, however, are a living proof that this is so. They experienced great joy as well as great suffering in their lives because they conformed themselves to the Cross of Christ. Pope Paul in his Apostolic Exhortation *Gaudete in Domino* has a whole section on "Joy in the hearts of the Saints" in which he shows that the saints testify to the truth that "the combat for the kingdom necessarily includes passing through a passion of love". The same principle holds for us all: "through the cross to the light (*per crucem ad lucem*), and from this world to the Father, in the life-giving breath of the Spirit".[5]

3   Scripture in Paschaltide

How does the Church present the word of God in this season? This we must now consider, since it is in the light of sacred Scripture that the liturgical commemorations of Christ's mysteries are most fully understood.

There is nothing haphazard about the choice of readings for this period. A careful study of the Lectionary reveals a carefully thought-out plan; and it is against this background that we can best appreciate the readings for a particular day.

With sure judgment the Church favours particular books of the New Testament for particular times of the year. This is part of her *didascalia* or teaching function which is exercised in a pre-eminent way in the liturgy.

In the selection and organisation of readings both for the Mass and Office, the Church has remained faithful to the centuries-old tradition of the Roman liturgy. There are new features, it is true, and a far greater number of readings than in the past, but no radical departures from ancient usage. For Christians today as in the past this provides a sure way to an understanding of the mysteries we celebrate. Through a prayerful use of these readings we will deepen our understanding of Christ, the Church and the Christian life.

The Gospel in Paschaltide

It is noteworthy that throughout the fifty days it is the gospel of St John which predominates. This is not by accident: the choice of the fourth evangelist is intentional. He is the one singled out to lead us through these weeks.

It is true that during the Easter octave the synoptic gospels are also read. On each day of the octave we are presented with a resurrection narrative. We hear the witness of Matthew, Mark, Luke and John. It is important that we should hear all four accounts. Each gospel is inspired and there is no question of one being more important than the other. Moreover each sheds a special light on the events of Easter Sunday.

Once the octave is over it is almost exclusively the voice of John that is heard. This is true of the Sundays and weekdays, although an exception must be made for the third Sunday and also for Ascension Day. Beginning with chapter three of this gospel there follows a semi-continuous reading terminating with the last verse of the final chapter on the eve of Pentecost Sunday.

Not all of St John's gospel is read at this time, but a very large portion of it. The Lectionary skips here and there, but sections of special catechetical importance, e.g., the discourses on the Bread of Life (ch. 6) and the Good Shepherd (ch. 10) are given in their entirety. Our Lord's final discourse, culminating in his great prayer for the Church, bring this gospel to a close.

Now this choice of St John for Paschaltide is deeply rooted in liturgical tradition. The Church has always seen a close affinity between this gospel and the season following Easter. This is certainly borne out by the history of the Roman rite, but it is witnessed to by other liturgical traditions as well, e.g. the Byzantine and Old Spanish rites.[1]

Why this preference for the fourth gospel at this high season of the Church's year? No doubt it is motivated by the realisation that St John sees more deeply into the mystery of Christ. What he has heard and seen and touched, his own experience of "the Word of life", this he shares with us. He is well named "the theologian" since he shows the mysteries hidden beneath the external events of Christ's life. He is as concerned about the facts of this life as are the other evangelists, but he is more conscious of their symbolic value. The miracles which Jesus performs are also "signs" pointing to other mysterious realities.

It may be said that St John sees the whole life-story of Jesus in the light of its fulfilment in the glory of Easter. The glow of the Resurrection lights up even the terrible events of Good Friday. The paschal mystery of the passion, death and resurrection of the Lord is present throughout the entire narrative.

St John has preserved more fully than the other sacred writers the words and discourses of Jesus. His final discourse at the Last Supper has been described as "the summit of revelation". These words were spoken by the Master before his return to the Father. Their full significance would be grasped only later:

> I still have many things to say to you
> but they would be too much for you now.
> But when the Spirit of truth comes he will
> lead you into all truth . . . *(Jn 16:12-13)*.

The Church, guided by the Holy Spirit, ponders over these words of Christ. They are proclaimed in the liturgy of Paschaltide and each year we discover new depths of meaning in them. We are thus led progressively into a fuller understanding of the mystery of Christ.

The Sunday gospels

The Sunday readings, including the gospels, follow an arrangement of their own. Here we consider the gospel readings for the Sundays between Easter and Pentecost.

On the second Sunday of Easter the gospel recounts the appearance of the Lord to the company of apostles including Thomas *(Jn 20:19-31)*. This occurred eight days later, that is on the octave day of Easter, and so the choice of this reading on this second Sunday requires no explanation. From the doctrinal point of view it has much to tell us about faith. It shows the victory of faith over doubt and mistrust. There is a doubting Thomas in each one of us, always requiring guarantees and reassurances. This must give way to a confident attitude of faith and trust. The apostle's belated but magnificent profession of faith must become our own: "My Lord and my God."

On the third Sunday the gospels are arranged according to the three-year cycle. The readings for years A and B are taken from St Luke's gospel *(Lk 24:13-35 and 35-48)*. The first extract describes how Jesus appeared to the two disciples on the road to Emmaus and how they recognised him in the breaking of bread. The next extract is a continuation of that chapter and sets the scene in the upper room in Jerusalem where again the Lord appears, speaks to his disciples and shares a meal with them. The gospel for year C is again from John *(Jn 21:1-19)*, and tells what happened by the shore of Lake Tiberias: how, after the miraculous catch of fish, the disciples recognise the Lord; they have a meal together and Peter receives his commission to "feed my lambs" and to "feed my sheep".

In each of these gospels there is an account of a meal which the Risen Lord has with his disciples. A meal expresses intimacy and fellowship. Christ, now returned to the Father, remains on terms of friendship and familiarity with his followers.

Nothing essential has changed in his relationship with them. The bond uniting Master and disciple has not been severed; rather has it been strengthened to make of that relationship a true communion.

This emphasis on the meal suggests another thought. The Eucharist is a sacred meal at which the Lord presides. It is "the Lord's Supper". We are his invited guests and we partake of his sacramental body and blood. It is a mystery of faith. We do not see the one who has invited us but through faith we recognise him in word and sacrament, in "the breaking of the bread".

The fourth Sunday is devoted to the Good Shepherd. It is "Good Shepherd Sunday". The gospel readings for the three years are all taken from the one great discourse *(Jn 10:1-30)*. The whole liturgy of this Sunday serves to highlight this central theme: opening prayer, second reading, responsorial psalm and alleluia verse as well as the communion antiphon and prayer after communion — all allude to Christ as the Good Shepherd.

For Christians of very early times this was the representation of Christ which attracted them most. We find it depicted in ancient places of worship, in the catacombs and elsewhere. Sometimes it is Christ shepherding his sheep in heavenly pastures. More often, it seems, it is a portrait of a young man carrying the lost sheep on his shoulders: the Good Shepherd of the synoptic gospels *(Mt 18:12-24; Lk 15:4-7).* The early Church responded to this image as Christians of much later times would respond to the symbol of the Sacred Heart.[2]

No gospel reading is more characteristic of the paschal season than that of the Good Shepherd. When we read and meditate upon it we find that all the great truths of our redemption are contained in it. Christ's atoning sacrifice is expressed in the image of the shepherd laying down his life for the sheep. The motivation of that sacrifice: loving obedience to the Father. Its final purpose: that they may have life in abundance.

The parable of the Good Shepherd shows us Christ at work in the Church in every age. From heaven he continues to pasture his flock. As one writer observes: "Since his passing over through death and resurrection, he has entered into glory with the Father, and it is from there that he leads his flock to perfection."[3]

Finally, it beautifully conveys the relationship between Christ and his Church and between Christ and each individual soul. How much is said in the phrase: "I know my own and my own know me"! Knowledge, in the biblical sense, has a rich connotation. It is something dynamic expressing itself in love and service of the other. It engages the heart as much as the mind. Christ's love for us is something intimate and personal; and our love for him is a response to his call: we hear his voice and we follow him. Such is the mutual knowledge of Shepherd and sheep.

The gospel readings for the fifth Sunday reveal other aspects of this relationship. Christ is "the

Way, the Truth and the Life", we are reminded in the gospel for year A *(Jn 14:1-12)*. Union with him is indispensable for supernatural life and growth; thus teaches the reading for year B *(Jn 15:1-8)*. Christ is the true vine and we are the branches. Union with him must be maintained at all costs. Suffering is a condition of growth: the vinedresser must prune the branches in order that they may bear more fruit. There is a theology of suffering here. The gospel text for year C *(Jn 13:31-35)* is about the "new commandment" to love one another. Christ's love for us is to be the measure of our love for one another.

The sixth Sunday prepares us for the coming feast of Pentecost. In the gospel for the first and third years Jesus promises the Holy Spirit and describes his role in the Church. He will be an Advocate and Teacher, leading the Church into all truth. He is the source of that love which is the great principle of unity in the Church.

This theme of unity is taken up on the final Sunday before Pentecost. The gospels are all from chapter 17 of St John's gospel which give us that great prayer sometimes known as "the High Priestly Prayer". In it Jesus implores the Father to keep the disciples true to his name and to maintain the Church in perfect unity.

Other New Testament readings

The reading of The Acts of the Apostles during

Paschaltide has also a long tradition behind it.
Beginning on Easter Sunday it is read each day at
Mass right up to Pentecost. An indication of its
importance is the fact that on the Sundays of this
season the first reading is not from the Old Testament, as is the general rule; instead we have a passage from Acts followed by another New Testament
reading. This is the time not of prophecy but of fulfilment and it is in the records of the first Christian
community that this fulfilment is manifested.

One could argue that the liturgical reading of
Acts should follow on the feast of Pentecost, an
arrangement more in keeping with the chronological
sequence. That is true, but it is only one consideration and not a major one. More important is it to
show how the way of life of the first Christian
communities was a living witness to the Resurrection. The Good News of the Resurrection is the
central message of the apostolic preaching. The
signs and wonders performed by the apostles con-
firm their message as does their readiness to suffer
persecution for Christ's sake.

Acts deals with the Church in its infancy, that
Church which was born from the side of Christ as
he "slept the sleep of death on the cross".[4] It is
appropriate that in this post-paschal season we
should relive that history of early development and
expansion. It portrays a Christian community sharing everything in common, in which there is but
"one heart and soul": a community striving to
live by the moral standards laid down by Christ;

a Church animated and led by the Holy Spirit.

St Luke, in this chronicle of the infant Church, describes a life of unceasing activity. Is there not a marked contrast between this and the gospel of St John, so serene and contemplative in character? This contrast underlines the twofold nature of the Church which is both active and contemplative, combining the roles of Martha and Mary. In the words of the Liturgy Constitution (art. 2): "The Church is essentially both human and divine, visible but endowed with invisible realities, zealous in action and dedicated to contemplation, present in the world, but as a pilgrim . . ."

The Liturgy of the Hours

The Breviary, in its office of readings, draws on other books of the New Testament to enrich our understanding of the paschal mystery in the life of the Church.

During the first week the scripture reading is from the First Letter of St Peter. The choice is admirable when one considers the pronounced baptismal character of this letter. Some commentators have even suggested that this is an Easter homily addressed to the newly-baptised.[5] This is disputed, however. Certainly in its opening section it reads like an exhortation to the newly-baptised to be faithful to their calling. It contains important doctrine on the nature of baptism: its regenerating effect which it derives from the paschal mystery of Christ; its corporate aspect, introducing its recipients into the people of God. Through baptism the life-giving power of the Resurrection is communicated to the neophyte.

The Book of Revelation or Apocalypse figures prominently in the office of readings, beginning on Monday of the second week and continuing until the end of the fifth week. It harmonises well with the liturgy of this time which celebrates the victory of Christ. This victory is the great theme of Revelation. Here we behold Christ in glory, having overcome all his enemies. He is depicted as the Lamb who has redeemed his people and will lead them to final victory. His struggle with the powers of darkness continues in the Church. In spite of unremitting persecution, final victory is assured. The book concludes with songs of victory in heaven and a vision of the New Jerusalem.

Finally, during the last two weeks of Paschaltide it is again the apostle John who addresses us in his letters to the churches. These writings, especially the first letter, correspond so well with chapters fifteen to seventeen of St John's gospel read at Mass during this time. The commandment to love one another as Christ has loved us is the great theme both of the gospel and of the letters. This commandment, both old and new, is of the essence of Christianity.

St John urges us to live in the spirit of baptismal renewal. This means breaking with sin, walking in the light of God's grace, keeping the commandments and remaining uncontaminated by the world. It implies living as befits our status of children of God. Love must be the hall-mark of our lives, love not in words only but in "deed and truth".

The great struggle between good and evil, so dramatically depicted in Revelation, has its counterpart in the letters. Here it is fought out not on the grand stage of world and cosmos, but in the very heart of man. Here Christ continues to do battle with Satan and to overcome. In this struggle, in which all of us are engaged, our weapons are the twin armoury of faith and love. Through faith we overcome and Christ's victory is ours: "Who can overcome the world? Only the man who believes that Jesus is the Son of God" *(Jn 5:5)*. Through the practice of love the paschal mystery of Christ becomes a reality in our lives: "We have passed out of death and into life, and of this we can be sure because we love our brothers" *(3:14)*.

4 Paschal sacraments

Paschaltide is a sacramental time. No study of its liturgy would be complete without some consideration of the sacraments. Here we consider the sacraments of baptism and the eucharist which, together with confirmation, constitute the rites of Christian initiation. They are by a special title, though not in an exclusive sense, paschal sacraments. If the other sacraments are less in evidence, they too derive their efficacy from the paschal mystery of Christ.

This unmistakable sacramental quality of the paschal liturgy has an historical explanation. It derives from the ancient discipline of the catechumenate. Our Lenten liturgy has preserved elements of baptismal instruction intended for the catechumens preparing for baptism at Easter.[1] This instruction consisted of an outline of salvation history together with a full exposition of the articles of faith summarised in the Apostles' Creed; also the basics of Christian morality.

Now once the rites of initiation (baptism, confirmation and eucharist) had been received, the process of formation was not at an end. There followed a period of post-baptismal instruction, the time of the "mystagogical catechesis". This was a kind of in-depth initiation into the meaning of the sacraments. In the fourth and fifth centuries a certain secrecy surrounded the Christian "mysteries" or sacraments. To preserve them from profanation by non-believers they were carefully guarded. Even the catechumens were not taught their full meaning and symbolism until after their baptism.

Paschaltide, and in particular the octave of Easter, was the time when the riches of the sacraments were explained to the neophytes. These new Christians were brought together frequently, even daily, to pray together and to receive instruction from the bishop or his representative. The sacred rites they had received on Easter night were explained in a series of homilies. This form of catechesis is known to us through such famous works as *The Mystagogical Catechesis*, attributed to St Cyril of Jerusalem, the Catechetical Homilies of St John Chrysostom and St Theodore of Mopsuestia, St Ambrose's *De Sacramentis* and St Augustine's many sermons to the newly-baptised.[2]

Now this instruction has relevance for Christians today as in the past, for newcomers to the faith, adult converts and for those baptised in infancy. In the school of the Lord's service we are all learners. During Lent the Church invites us to join the catechumens preparing for baptism. During Paschaltide we join the neophytes: with them we learn from the liturgy all that the sacraments should mean for Christian men and women. This can lead to a renewal and deepening of our sacramental life.[3]

The commemoration of baptism

The liturgy of the Easter octave has many baptismal motifs. In fact it would seem that the octave was originally conceived as an octave of baptism; later, about the seventh century, it was organised more specifically as an octave of the resurrection. That is why the octave concluded on Easter Saturday, the day when the neophytes laid aside their white garments and returned to secular life.[4]

Let us now examine the texts of the missal and lectionary to see how they recall the sacrament of baptism in the celebration of the eucharist.

First, the entrance antiphons for each day of Easter week shed their own light on baptism. It is in the imagery of the Old Testament, especially of the Book of Exodus, that they present it. Through baptism we join God's people in their great exodus, we pass over from slavery to freedom; with Christ, the new Moses, at our head, we journey on to the promised land. Already, through baptism and eucharist, we have entered that promised land; we have accepted Christ's invitation: "Come, you whom my Father has blessed; inherit the kingdom prepared for you since the foundation of the world, alleluia" (antiphon for Easter Wednesday, from *Mt 25:34*).

We should not overlook a rite of great interest even though it is an optional element in the Mass. I refer to the ceremony of the blessing and sprinkling of holy water. This may take the place of the penitential rite at the beginning of Mass. During Easter Time its baptismal symbolism is underlined. There is a special prayer of blessing, at the conclusion of which the priest says: "May this water remind us of our baptism and let us share the joy of all who have been baptised at Easter."

Having blessed the water, the celebrant may now proceed down the church sprinkling the people with this sacramental. During the procession an appropriate song is sung. What could be more appropriate than the traditional chant of *Vidi aquam*? In English it is rendered: "I saw water flowing from the right side of the temple, alleluia. It brought God's life and his salvation, and the people sang in joyful praise: alleluia, alleluia" *(see Ezek 47:1-2, 9)*.

Jesus spoke of his own body as a temple *(see Jn 2:19-22);* and it was from the pierced side of that temple that there flowed blood and water *(Jn 19:34),* symbolising redemption and, according to the fathers of the Church, the sacraments of baptism and eucharist.

In representations of Christ on the cross, the sword-thrust is shown on the right hand of the body, although the heart is on the left side. This shows the influence of scripture and liturgy on Christian art. The underlying idea is that Christ's body is the true temple and that in his passion he fulfils the prophecy of Ezechiel. [5]

An alternative antiphon expresses the same thought in more explicit terms: "Lord Jesus, from your wounded side flowed streams of cleansing waters: the world was washed of all its sin, all life made new again, alleluia."

The opening prayer at Mass, which is also the prayer said at the liturgical hours, has frequent allusions to baptism. In these prayers the Church frequently asks that the grace received in baptism may become manifest in our lives. Let us quote one example:

> Lord God, you increase day by day the number of your Church's children born in the waters of baptism. Grant that your people may hold fast in life to the mystery of new birth which they received by faith. (Monday of Easter Octave, Breviary version.)

The readings at Mass also relate to baptism. The Acts of the Apostles recount many instances of baptism and the outpouring of the Holy Spirit. The responsorial psalm sometimes has a baptismal theme as, for example, Psalm 41 with its response "My soul is thirsting for God, the God of my life." The Gospel readings have less direct bearing on baptism because during Lent some of the great Johannine discourses, understood in a baptismal sense, have already been read.[6] But included in the liturgy of the word for Monday and Tuesday of the second week is Christ's discourse with Nicodemus *(Jn 3:1-15)* in which he speaks of the necessity of being born again "through water and the spirit".

Before leaving the Mass some mention should be made of a reference to baptism inside the eucharistic prayer itself. It is found in Eucharistic Prayer 1 (Roman Canon) and is said each day of the octave. It speaks of the newly-baptised and the privilege which is now theirs of being able to share in the Church's sacrifice:

> Father, accept this offering from your whole family and from those born into the new life of water and the Holy Spirit, with all their sins forgiven . . .

The Mass or Eucharist is the sacrifice of Christ and of his Church. Through baptism the faithful are enabled to participate in that sacrifice. Not only may they receive the body and blood of the Lord, but they too share in the oblation, "offering the immaculate victim, not only through the hands of the priest but also together with him".[7] This is the doctrine of the general priesthood of the faithful (as distinct from the ministerial priesthood), which underlies so much of recent liturgical reforms.

The patristic readings of the Divine Office also teach about baptism and contain much of value. Two of the homilies for the octave (Thursday and Friday) are from the *Mystagogical Catechesis* already referred to. In the first instruction *(Divine Office 11,* pp. 404-5) the homilist describes how baptism draws us into the mysteries of Christ's death and resurrection. He exclaims:

> What a strange and astonishing situation! We did not really die, we were not really buried, we did not really hang from a cross and rise again. Our imitation was symbolic, but *our salvation a reality.*

In the second instruction (pp. 415-17), he treats of the anointing of the Holy Spirit and of our being conformed to Christ. "Since you share in Christ," he says, "it is right to call you 'Christs' or anointed ones." And, having explained the symbolism of the anointing with oil, he declares: "The body is anointed with visible ointment, and the soul is sanctified by the holy, hidden Spirit."

On the Sunday after Easter it is the great pastoral bishop, Augustine, who addresses us. The reading is from a sermon he gave to the newly-baptised on the octave of their baptism. There is in his words a note of tenderness and concern for these new Christians whom he has carefully trained. He exhorts them to be true to their calling, to "put on the Lord Jesus" and to persevere in the new life, confident that one day they would receive the glory of the resurrection.

Another baptismal instruction provides the reading for Wednesday of the third week of Easter. It is from the first Apology of St Justin Martyr, who wrote this treatise probably in Rome at the beginning of the second century. It is of interest on account of its great antiquity and because of the information it gives us about the administration of the sacraments at such an early time. He speaks of baptism as a "consecration", a spiritual birth, and as an "enlightening" — this latter being the name given to the sacrament in the early Church.

Finally, on Monday of the sixth week *(Divine Office 11*, pp. 607-8) we have an extract from a fourth century treatise on the Blessed Trinity by Didymus of Alexandria. This great lay theologian describes the activity of the Holy Spirit in baptism:

> He frees us from sin and death; and from being earthy, made of dust and ashes, he makes us spiritual, sharers in the divine glory, sons and heirs of our God and Father, formed according to the image of the Son, his fellow heirs and his brothers, who will reign with him and share his glory.

The Eucharist

Baptism gives access to the Eucharist, the sacrament which completes Christian initiation. (Confirmation formerly preceded first communion; it was administered immediately after baptism.) Our incorporation with Christ is begun at baptism, it is completed by our participation in the eucharist. Through baptism and confirmation we are drawn into the paschal mystery of Christ; the eucharist completes our insertion into that mystery. Thus the three sacraments of initiation form a unity, even if they are administered at different stages of a person's life.

The paschaltide liturgy has valuable elements of eucharistic teaching. These deserve to be brought to the notice of the faithful. Much of this teaching is to be found in the breviary and so is not available to the generality of lay Christians. The pastoral clergy ought to bring to their people some of the riches they have assimilated in the liturgy. The period between Easter and Pentecost would be an excellent occasion to preach on the sacraments of Christian initiation.

Let us first look at the gospel readings at Mass. St John, unlike the other evangelists, has not left an account of the institution of the eucharist. There is, none the less, a strong sacramental emphasis in his gospel. The mystery of the eucharist is certainly to be found there.

It is in chapter six of St John's gospel that we will find our Lord's teaching about the eucharist. This chapter treats of the miracle of the multiplication of bread, followed by Christ's great discourse on the Bread of Life. On Friday of the second week we read of the multiplication of bread *(Jn 6:1-15)*. This miracle foreshadows the eucharist, as St Augustine and other of the Church fathers like to explain. It provides the occasion for the discourse which follows.

From Monday to Saturday of the third week, there is read each day an extract from this discourse. Jesus leads his hearers from their preoccupation with material bread to deeper, more spiritual realities. He declares that he himself is "the true bread":

I am the bread of life.
He who comes to me will never be hungry;
he who believes in me will never thirst.

Faith in him is a God-given gift; it is to be "drawn by the Father". To come to Christ by faith and love is to have the assurance of eternal life: "I will raise him up on the last day."

As the discourse draws to a conclusion, we move, almost imperceptibly, to a consideration of Christ's eucharistic presence. How can we interpret his words other than in terms of a real presence in the sacrament? For he said: "My flesh is real food and my blood is real drink. He who eats my flesh and drinks my blood lives in me and I live in him."

At this point we may turn to the patristic readings of the breviary. It is remarkable how their writings remain faithful to the teaching of Christ. The doctrine of the Real Presence is clearly witnessed to in their instructions on the eucharist. The office of readings for Paschaltide contains at least seven patristic homilies treating of the eucharistic mystery.[8]

Two of these are the work of second century authors, St Justin Martyr and St Irenaeus. Both insist on the reality of Christ's presence in the eucharist. For the former it is "the flesh and blood of this Jesus who became flesh"; and the latter declares that when the bread and wine re-

ceive God's word "they become the eucharist, the
body and blood of Christ".

St Hilary, in an extract from his work *De Trinitate*,
also affirms the Real Presence. He develops a point
of doctrine arising out of this, namely that the
grace of the sacrament is operative even outside the
time of communion. Through faith and love Christ's
presence in the heart of the believer is an abiding
one, and this presence is maintained, the union
between Christ and the soul is deepened, by means
of the eucharist. St Hilary is but echoing our Lord's
words when he says: "If the Word was truly made
flesh and if we truly receive the Word made flesh
in the Lord's food, why should we not hold that he
remains within us naturally?"

The eucharist is the sacrament of the unity of
the Church. This is a thought often dwelt upon by
the Church fathers. According to St Fulgentius, a
sixth century North African bishop: "The spiritual
building-up of the body of Christ is brought about
by love . . . It is never carried out more purpose-
fully than when the Church (which is itself Christ's
body) offers his body and blood under the signs
of bread and wine" (*Divine Office 11*, p. 511).

Pope St Leo possessed a deep sense of the
Church as the Body of Christ. He never thought of
Christ in separation from the Church. For him "the
head cannot be separated from the members, nor
can the members from the head". In the course of
his reflections on the presence of Christ in his
Church, in a homily read on Wednesday of the

second week (p. 515), he introduces the subject of the eucharist. He shows that the effect produced in those who receive this sacrament is to be changed into the One whom they receive:

> For our participation in the body and blood of Christ has this effect: it makes us become what we receive; it enables us, with our whole being, in our spirit and our flesh, to bear him in whom and with whom we have died and been buried and risen again.

These are some of the themes of eucharistic doctrine found in the patristic readings of Paschal-tide. In reading them we find our faith strengthened and our understanding enriched. This should lead to a renewal and intensification of our sacramental life.

5   Ascension into glory

"He ascended into heaven." This is one of the articles of faith which we profess in the Creed. It is included among the glorious mysteries of the Rosary and has its place in the *anamnesis* or memorial prayer of the Mass. On this day the Church celebrates the Ascension with full solemnity.

This feast was instituted in the course of the fourth century. It commemorates the event described in The Acts of the Apostles *(1:1-11)*. The scene is set on the Mount of Olives just forty days after the resurrection. Jesus appears for the last time to his disciples. He entrusts them with a great mission: they are to be his witnesses, preaching the Good News throughout the entire world. They would be strengthened for their task by the Holy Spirit. Having thus spoken and given his final instructions, he was taken up to heaven. Two angels appear promising the disciples that Jesus would return one day in the same way they had seen him depart.

This summarises St Luke's account of the ascension in Acts. It is this account which provides the first reading of the Mass and may be regarded

as the principal text of today's feast. The synoptic
gospels also record this event. St Matthew does not
actually speak of an ascension *(28:16-20)*, but he
describes a final meeting between Jesus and his
disciples in Galilee when Peter and his companions
receive their mission to the world. St Mark briefly
describes the ascension at the end of his gospel
(16:14-20). He simply records the fact that the
Lord Jesus was "taken up to heaven" and that "at
the right hand of God he took his place". St Luke
in his gospel *(24:50-53)*, leaves us a beautiful
picture of Jesus with raised hands blessing his disciples at the very moment of his departure. Here,
in contrast with his account in Acts, the ascension
seems to take place on Easter day itself.

In the course of the three-year cycle the gospels
of Matthew, Mark and Luke are read. Each evangelist sheds a light on the mystery we are celeb-
rating. St John has no parallel account, but he does
record the words of the risen Lord to Mary
Magdalene: "I am ascending to my Father and
your Father, to my God and your God" *(Jn 20:17)*.

Resurrection and Ascension are distinct mysteries
which in God's plan of salvation are intimately
related. Christ's exaltation, begun on Easter Sunday,
became definitive and was fully manifested on
Ascension Day; then was his victory complete. As
one commentator remarks: "Resurrection and
exaltation form one, single paschal mystery of
Christ's victory over sin and death."[1]

The human mind needs visual images. The

imagination has a role to play in the development of religious knowledge. Christ in his teaching made frequent use of images and parables. The Ascension lends itself to pictorial representation and has inspired many great works of art. We need not fear to use our imaginations to visualise the Resurrection and Ascension. Let us bear in mind, however, that no image or representation can adequately express the mystery itself. The mysteries of Christ cannot be grasped by the senses alone.

There are other scriptural texts which the liturgy sets before us this day. There are the psalms which evoke the mystery and celebrate its triumph, as does psalm 46 in Mass and Office: "God goes up with shouts of joy, the Lord goes up with trumpet blast." St Paul made much use of psalm 67 in his Letter to the Ephesians and develops a theology of the ascension from a verse of the psalm which he quotes: "When he ascended to the height, he captured prisoners, he gave gifts to men." The Letter to the Ephesians is read both at the office of readings and at Mass.

We do not meet the word "ascension" very often in the New Testament, but the reality which that word expresses is implied in such phrases as "taken up in glory", "seated at God's right hand". Resurrection, exaltation, enthronement at God's right hand — these are spoken of simultaneously in so much of St Paul and the other New Testament writers.

In the Letter to the Hebrews the mystery of the

ascension is contemplated from another angle. Christ's entry into heaven is presented as the entry of the High Priest into the sactuary. It is as our mediator and high priest that he enters into the presence of his Father. We may here quote from one of the passages of scripture given for the midday office:

> This high priest of ours is one who has taken his seat in heaven, on the right hand of that throne where God sits in majesty, ministering now in the sactuary, in that true tabernacle which the Lord, not man, has set up *(Heb 8:1-3)*.

These passages of scripture, and there are many others, all converge on the one mystery. They offer so many approaches to an understanding of the saving event which the Church is commemorating today. No single text of scripture should be taken in isolation, but should be studied and reflected on in conjunction with other texts which also have a bearing on the mystery. This is the method of the liturgy and it is one from which we can all learn.

The Ascension and human destiny

Let us now consider how the ascension affects our own destinies as individuals and as members of the Church. That the ascension of Christ is also *ours* is one of the principal ideas of today's feast. Our share in this mystery is a cause of unbounded hope.

By his ascension "the human nature of the risen Christ has been taken into the sphere of divine life with the Father, Son and Holy Spirit in power and majesty".[2] And since we all share one human nature, it may be said that humanity has entered with Christ into the glory of heaven. Our mortal nature is there with Christ, if not yet fully at least *in principle*. And not only human nature but in a sense *all creation* is included in that ascension. Exalted above the heavens, Christ has *filled all things* with his presence. Everything in the universe has come into contact with the risen Christ.

But it is with the Church, the Body of Christ, that St Paul is most concerned. The Church is "the fullness of him who fills the whole creation" *(Ep 1:23)*. In the unity of one body, head and members cannot be separated. This thought, so basic to St Paul's understanding of the Church, has inspired much of today's liturgy. Let us now illustrate this.

The hymn for evening prayer in its first strophe announces this theme:

> The Lord goes up with shouts of joy,
> while trumpets all his triumph tell;
> *with him humanity is raised*
> above angelic world to dwell.

In the Person of the Word incarnate, mankind enters into the sphere of the Blessed Trinity. This thought, so apt to inspire us with hope, has suggested the petition of the prayer which concludes each liturgical hour:

> Almighty God,
> fill us with a holy joy,
> teach us how to thank you with reverence and love
> on account of the ascension of Christ your Son.
> You have raised us up with him:
> where he, the head, has preceded us in glory,
> there we, the body, are called in hope.

This fine prayer is inspired by a sermon of Pope St Leo the Great. In one of his sermons on the ascension we find the phrase: "Where he, the head, has preceded us in glory, there we, the body, are called in hope."[3] He goes on to say that not only have we become possessors of paradise through Christ's ascension but that we have penetrated the heights of heaven in Christ.

In the office of readings for this feast, St Augustine proposes a similar train of thought. At the beginning of his discourse he observes: "Just as he ascended without leaving us, so too we are already with him in heaven, although his promises have not yet been fulfilled in our bodies." He then exhorts us to be even more closely joined to Christ through faith, hope, love and desire. St Augustine, like St Leo, was absorbed by the doctrine of the Mystical Body which they found in the writings of

St Paul. At the conclusion of his homily St
Augustine summarises his own thought in a lapidary
phrase: "That is why no one has descended but
Christ, and no one but Christ has ascended." For
this father of the Church, "Christ is many members
but one body".

We follow this theme through the Mass. In the
first preface for the feast the Church thanks the
Father for this mystery of salvation in which
human hope is grounded:

> Christ, the mediator between God and man,
> judge of the world and Lord of all,
> has passed beyond our sight,
> not to abandon us but to be our hope.
> Christ is the beginning, the head of the
>   Church;
> where he has gone, we hope to follow.

Here again we meet the thought of Christ's
ascension being also the Church's ascension because
of the unity of head and members. We also meet
another idea, to be developed later, that Christ,
while visibly departing from his Church, has not
abandoned it. In his own words: "I am going now
to prepare a place for you", and " I will not leave
you orphans" (*Jn 14:2* and *18*). This idea is taken
up in the second preface which alludes to our
Lord's promise that he is going to prepare a place
for us and "to claim for us a share in his divine
life".

The Roman canon receives an insertion on this

day commemorating the mystery of the ascension
and presenting it in terms of the indissoluble union
of head and members:

> In union with the whole Church we celebrate
> that day when Christ, your only Son, our
> Lord, took his place with you and raised our
> frail human nature to glory.

The eucharist is our *viaticum* (food for the
journey). In our following of Christ to glory we
have the sacraments, especially the eucharist, to
help us along the way. Christ promised eternal life
to those who would eat his flesh and drink his
blood, and added that he would raise them up on
the last day (cf. *Jn 6:54*). This sacrament then is
the God-given means by which we can achieve our
eternal destiny. This thought is suggested in the
prayer over the gifts: "May his gifts help us to rise
with him to the joys of heaven"; and in the prayer
after communion a similar idea is expressed: "Help
us to follow Christ with love to eternal life where
he is Lord for ever and ever."

The Church's mission

We ought not overlook the missionary aspect of
this feast. Before his ascension Christ entrusted his
disciples with a tremendous mission: to prolong
among all the nations of the earth his own saving
work for mankind. They were to be his witnesses
"throughout Judaea and Samaria and indeed to the

ends of the earth" *(Acts 1:8)*. They were to "go therefore, make disciples of all nations" *(Mt 28:19)*; and they were to remember that "repentance for the forgiveness of sins would be preached to all the nations" *(Lk 24:47)*.

A daunting prospect for a small band of men, none of whom had shown heroism at the time of Christ's passion; at the hour of trial even Peter failed him. A daunting prospect too for the Church of our day which, in comparison with the total population of the world is indeed a "little flock"; and if we estimate the size of the Church not in terms of mere numbers but in terms of those who are Christians in deed as well as in name, then we are completely outnumbered.

But with the mission goes a solemn promise: "I am with you always; yes, to the end of time." This promise has fortified the Church down through the centuries. In the midst of persecution the people of God have remembered this promise and in their sufferings have experienced the presence and the power of the risen and ascended Lord.

This promise of Christ's abiding presence is echoed through the Mass: in the first reading, in the alleluia verse and at the conclusion of the gospel. We hear it again in the communion antiphon. And last of all, in the solemn blessing for this day:

> You believe that Jesus has taken his seat in majesty at the right hand of the Father. May you have the joy of experiencing that he is

also with you to the end of time according to
his promise.

6 Presence and promise

The abiding presence

It was once the custom for the deacon or other minister to extinguish the paschal candle after the reading of the gospel on Ascension Day. This signified Christ's bodily ascension after the forty days and his return to the Father. This is no longer the case in the reformed liturgy. The candle continues to be lit each day at Mass until the end of the paschal season. It is not removed from the sanctuary until the conclusion of the liturgy of Pentecost. Even then it is not removed from the church but placed in the baptistry to be used whenever the sacrament of re-birth is administered; it thus symbolises the continued presence of Christ in the sacraments.

In the days between Ascension and Pentecost, the thought of Christ's enduring presence in the Church pervades the whole liturgy. This presence is very much bound up with the coming of the Holy Spirit. At the Last Supper Jesus promised: "I will not leave you orphans, I will come back to you" *(Jn 14: 18);* and he said: "I am going away and shall return" *(Jn 14: 28)*. Mysterious words which seem to imply an imminent return. Between Pasch and Parousia Jesus will be present to his people through the indwelling Spirit.

St John says: "We know that he lives in us by the Spirit that he has given us"*(1 Jn 3: 24)*. The apostle develops this thought in chapter four of this letter which is read on the Sunday following the Ascension (Year B). How beautifully the prayer for this Sunday expresses the longing for a more deeply felt awareness of the presence of Christ within us:

> Lord God, we believe that the Saviour of mankind is enthroned with you in majesty. Listen to our prayer, and, according to his promise, let us feel his presence among us until the end of time.

With the coming of the Holy Spirit, Christ is even more present to his people than he was when he was visibly present on earth. He is seen and recognised with the eyes of faith, a perception more sure than that of bodily vision. St Ignatius of Antioch has admirably expressed this in the words: "For good does not reside in what our eyes see; the fact that Jesus Christ is now with the Father is why we perceive him so much the more clearly."[1]

St Cyril of Alexandria discourses in a similar vein in his commentary on St John's gospel, an extract of which is given for the office of readings on Thursday following the Ascension. Speaking of

Christ and on the accomplishment of the mission entrusted to him by the Father, he observes: "Since the time and the need were now calling him to be carried to his Father in heaven, it was necessary for him to be present through the Spirit with those who worshipped him, and to dwell in our hearts through faith. Having him within us in this way, we would be able to cry out with confidence: 'Abba, Father.'" One has the impression in reading this passage that Cyril experienced in his own prayer-life what he so eloquently expresses in his writings.

The most remarkable patristic reading of all is that given for the Friday following the Ascension.[2] It is from a sermon of Pope St Leo. In it he explains how Christ's ascension increased the faith of the apostles; how from that moment they began to see him in a new way with minds and hearts enlightened by the light of faith:

> They fixed their minds on Christ's godhead as he sat on his Father's right hand. The evidence of their eyes no longer held back their mental vision from contemplating this truth, that the Son descended from his Father without leaving him, and ascended from his disciples without departing from them.

One is rather taken aback by the vigour and boldness of St Leo's thought. He seems to imply that the visible presence could be a hindrance to a fuller knowledge through faith of Christ's divine nature. And then he goes on to declare that the Son of God is more truly present after his ascension than before:

> For the Son of man, dearly beloved, was revealed more perfectly and solemnly as the Son of God once he had returned to the glory of his Father's majesty, and in a mysterious way he began to be more present to them in his godhead once he had become more distant in his humanity.

In this sermon St Leo also alludes to Christ's sacramental presence in a famous phrase: "The visible presence of our Redeemer passed over into sacraments; and so that faith might be more noble and firmer, it is grounded now not on sight but on doctrine."

This sacramental presence applies with special force to the eucharist. There Christ is present really and substantially, and not just by his power. And his presence is an abiding one continuing outside the Mass in the Blessed Sacrament. He is, as the name Emmanuel implies, "God with us". This is a mystery which the Church will soon be contemplating in the feast of *Corpus (et sanguis) Christi*.

The idea of "meeting Christ" in the sacraments is a traditional one. It finds beautiful expression in a passage from St Ambrose in which he exclaims: "You have revealed yourself to me face to face, O Christ; *I find you in the sacraments (in tuis te invenio sacramentis)*."[3] St Ephraem, too, speaks of meeting and even "welcoming" Christ in the sacraments.[4]

Present through the Holy Spirit, present in the sacraments, Christ thus realises his promise to be with his Church always. And these two modes of his presence are closely connected. For it is by the action of the Holy Spirit that the sacraments are efficacious signs of grace, and it is by the power of that same Spirit, invoked at the epiclesis of the Mass, that bread and wine are changed into the body and blood of Christ, and that we, members of Christ, become more fully his Mystical Body.

Promise of the Spirit

Pentecost is prepared for by prayer. So it was with the first Christian Pentecost. We read in Acts *(1:14)* that the disciples, after the ascension, devoted themselves to continuous prayer as they awaited the advent of the Holy Spirit: "All these joined in continuous prayer, together with several women, including Mary the mother of Jesus, and with his brothers." This scene is repeated in the Church's preparation for the feast of Pentecost; as this great solemnity approaches, all Christians are united in praying for a new outpouring of the Spirit of God in the Church. We invoke the intercession of Mary who was present at that first assembly on Pentecost morning.

Expectation of the Holy Spirit has been present throughout the whole paschal season, but becomes more emphatic and vocal from Ascension onwards. The Magnificat antiphon for second Evening Prayer on Ascension Day reminds the risen Jesus of the promise he made before his departure:

> King of glory, Lord almighty, today you have ascended victoriously above the heavens; do not leave us orphans without a guide, but send the one whom you promised, the gift of the Father, the Spirit of truth, alleluia.

Until the recent reform of the calendar the feast of Pentecost had an octave (terminating with Trinity Sunday). This has now gone, not because Pentecost is less important but because the Church wants to maintain the unity of the paschal season. Pentecost is the completion and the culmination of the great paschal solemnity extending over a period of seven weeks. The emphasis is no longer on an extension of the feast of Pentecost but rather on an intensive preparation for it. We now have a kind of octave in reverse. Some of the traditional prayers we associate with the old octave are now found in the days preceding the feast.

The days between Ascension and Pentecost are days of waiting and preparation. There is so much in the liturgy of the Mass and office to keep us in mind of the coming feast. In the entrance and communion antiphons of the Mass we hear our Lord's own words foretelling the advent of the Paraclete. The same is true for the alleluia verses which are proper to this time. Most of these are taken from chapters fourteen to sixteen of St John's gospel. As Christ comes to address us in the gospel reading, we acclaim him in his own words, as in the following: "Alleluia, alleluia! I will send you the spirit of truth, says the Lord; he will lead you to the complete truth."

The opening prayer of the Mass is addressed to the Father, asking him to fill his Church with the gift of his Spirit; or to strengthen us by the power of that Spirit to do his will and to be faithful to him; to make us temples of his glory; to unite the Church in the Holy Spirit; to make our hearts pleasing to him; to strengthen our faith. These are some of the thoughts expressed in these traditional prayers. They are simple, direct and at the same time profound. They make us conscious of the role of the Holy Spirit in our lives.

In the Divine Office we find the same emphasis. In the intercessions of the morning and evening offices, the Church is praying for the light and grace and strength of the second Divine Person. These intercessions are addressed to Christ and they express in more expanded form what the Roman collect states concisely. The grace of the Holy Spirit is asked for in a multiplicity of ways, and after each petition there is an appropriate response, such as: "May your Spirit come to our aid."

In the readings of the office, the fathers of the Church offer their own profound thoughts on the Spirit of God whom we have received at baptism and who is ever at work in our lives, distributing his gifts, leading us into all truth, and to that perfect unity which is the fruit of perfect love.

7 Pentecost Sunday

"The Spirit of the Lord fills the whole world!" It is Pentecost Sunday and the Church rejoices. Nature joins in the celebration: the burgeoning of new life at Easter has now grown to a profusion of blossom and foliage. Spring has reached its zenith and now ushers in the early summer.

Pentecost, or Whit Sunday, is a much loved feast. The splendour of its liturgy is exemplified by the words and music of those two masterpieces, the hymn *Veni Creator Spiritus* and the sequence *Veni Sancte Spiritus*, the one sung at vespers, the other at Mass. Both are addressed to the Holy Spirit, invoked as the Creator and Sanctifier.

Today's solemnity commemorates the events of the first Pentecost, so vividly described by St Luke in Acts *(2:1-11)*. This account provides the first reading of the Mass. We are all familiar with that scene in the upper room in Jerusalem: the little group of disciples suddenly disturbed by a powerful wind; then the appearance of tongues of fire which rested on each apostle; the speaking in foreign languages and the rapid conversion of many onlookers. These are the phenomena which announced the coming of the Holy Spirit at the first Pentecost.

The Church not only recalls this event, but relives it in the liturgical mystery. The Spirit, which "hovered over the waters" at the beginning of creation, the Spirit which appeared as wind and fire on the first Pentecost morning, continues to come and to shape the lives and destinies of men. In every age the Church has experienced the powerful presence and gentle influence of the Spirit. Today the Church celebrates that coming liturgically and prays that he will continue to come, to renew the face of the earth and to kindle in human hearts the fire of his love.

In this present time Pentecost has acquired a relevance and actuality greater than ever before. The second Vatican Council laid the foundation for a greater awareness of the Holy Spirit in the life of the Church and in the life of each Christian. We have now more in common with our brethren of the Eastern Church who always had a strong devotion to the Holy Spirit. We may thank them for having recalled us to this devotion.

Every great movement in the Church may be ascribed to the Holy Spirit. Pope Pius XII described the liturgical movement as the "breath of the Holy Spirit in the Church". The same could be said of the ecumenical movement, which is drawing Christians together in unity. The charismatic movement shows signs that here too the Spirit is at work, preparing what Cardinal Suenens describes as "a new Pentecost".[1]

From Jewish Pentecost to Christian feast

Some knowledge of the Old Testament background helps our understanding of the Church's feast of Pentecost. While its content is completely new — the descent of the Holy Spirit — there is, none the less, a certain relationship with the Jewish feast which it is important to understand.

For one thing, the name is the same. The word Pentecost (from the Greek *pentekoston* = the number 50) refers in both cases to a feast of the fiftieth day. For the Jews it was and continues to be the feast which follows fifty days after the Azymes or feast of Unleavened Bread. It was a feast of the harvest and comprised an offering of the first fruits to Yahweh. The harvest lasted seven weeks. The feast of Azymes, the day following the Passover, celebrated the beginning of the barley harvest and there was on this day an initial offering of the first sheaf; but the real harvest feast, when the cereal offerings were solemnly presented to the Lord, was the feast of Pentecost. This was one of the great feasts of pilgrimage for the Jewish people.

Our feast takes place fifty days after Easter, and the period between is one of continuous celebration. The idea of harvest and first fruits can be applied both to Easter and Pentecost. Does not St Paul speak of Jesus as the "first fruits" of redeemed humanity: "the first-fruits of all who have fallen asleep" *(1 Co 15:20)*. His resurrection took place when the first sheafs of corn were being offered in the Temple. The feast of Pentecost, seven weeks later, has also the character of a harvest feast. It is then the Holy Spirit descends like a fire to ripen the remainder of the corn and complete the harvest. This image of the harvest is certainly in the minds of the early fathers. St Irenaeus comments: "For the Spirit brought the scattered races together into a unity, and offered to the Father the first fruits of all the nations."[2] On Pentecost Day the Holy Spirit descended on the community of Christ's followers, producing a harvest of love; for, as St Paul says, "the fruit of the Spirit is love, joy, peace, patience, kindness, goodness, faithfulness, gentleness, self-control" *(Gal 5:22-23)*.

There is another aspect of the Jewish feast which can be of help to us. As well as being a feast of the harvest, it was also considered as a feast which commemorated the giving of the Law to Moses on Mount Sinai.[3] The emphasis was not so much on the giving of the Law as on the covenant entered upon between God and his people on that occasion. This notion of law and covenant — the new law and the new covenant — also enters into the Christian conception of Pentecost. The sending of the Holy Spirit replaces the promulgation of the Law. He is the "Finger of God", writing now not on tablets of stone but on human hearts. The covenant, established on the Mosaic law, is superseded by a new covenant which is based on the presence and action of the Spirit within us. It rests not just on adherence to an external code of conduct, but on an inner disposition of mind and heart, a "transformation from within". This law is a law of love, a principle of life. Pentecost may be considered then as a feast of the New Law and the New Covenant, promulgated by the Holy Spirit.

Pentecost and Easter

The coming of the Holy Spirit at Pentecost is consequent on the glorification of the Saviour. This glorification is manifested, above all, in his ascension. It was necessary that Christ should return to the Father, through the path of death and resurrection, before the Spirit could be sent. Jesus said: "Unless I go, the Advocate will not come to you" *(Jn 16: 17).*

St Peter, addressing the crowds at the first Pentecost, declared: "Now raised to the heights by God's right hand, he has received from the Father the Holy Spirit, who was promised, and what you see and hear is the outpouring of that Spirit"*(Acts 2: 33).*

There are several other passages expressing this relationship. Fr Robert Cabié has studied and compared them in his book *La Pentecôte* and comes to the following conclusion: "The gift of the Spirit is therefore inseparable from the exaltation of the Lord, together constituting the achievement of the redemptive work and inaugurating the new era which prepares for the Parousia."[4]

Completing the Paschal Mystery

Pentecost was sometimes designated as "the seal". Now a seal completes and authenticates a letter or document. Pentecost completes the mystery of redemption; it puts the seal to Christ's redeeming work. St Paul alludes to the Holy Spirit as the seal (*sphragis*), as in Ephesians *(1:13)*: " . . . you too have been stamped with the seal of the Holy Spirit of the Promise, . . ."

This idea of completion is given expression in the liturgy. We find it, first of all, in the prayer of the day (breviary version):

> Almighty, ever-living God,
> you ordained that the paschal mystery
> be *completed by the mystery of Pentecost.*
> Gather together, by your gift of grace,
> the scattered nations and divided tongues
> to one faith in your name.

The same thought is expressed in the preface of the Mass:

> Today you sent the Holy Spirit on those marked out to be your children by sharing the life of your only Son, and so you *brought the paschal mystery to its completion.*

And, finally, we meet it in one of the antiphons of the office: "Send forth your power, Lord, from your holy temple in Jerusalem, and bring to perfection your work among us, Alleluia!"

These considerations help us to see Pentecost in

a Christological light. This is also the impression
made on us by the gospel reading from St John
(20:19-23). Here the Risen Lord appears to his
disciples, wishes them peace and shows them his
hands and side. He entrusts them with their mission,
and then "after saying this he breathed on them
and said: 'Receive the Holy Spirit. . . .' " This
situates today's feast in the context of Easter, and
helps us to view the mysteries of the passion,
resurrection and descent of the Holy Spirit as a
unified whole.

The Father's gift

"There is a variety of gifts but always the same
Spirit", says St Paul in the second reading of the
Mass *(1 Co 12:3-7, 12-13)*. The Church acknow-
ledges these gifts and gives thanks to God for them.
Before we consider these gifts individually, let us
bear in mind that the Holy Spirit is greater than all
these gifts and is himself the Father's gift.

The Holy Spirit is, in the words of the hymn,
"the Gift of the Almighty God" *(donum Dei
altissimi)*. St Luke in his gospel *(11:13)*, recalls
that the gift of the Holy Spirit will be given to
those who humbly ask the heavenly Father for it.
The Holy Spirit is God's gift whom we received in
baptism, and whose temples we are. The individual
gifts, so diverse in character, are simply manifestations of his presence.

The prayer of the liturgy is that we may possess

this gift more fully. "Fill us with the gift of your Spirit", asks the prayer for Saturday after the Ascension; and on Friday of the following week we say: "May our sharing in this gift increase our love and make our faith grow stronger." And in this context we may also recall the words of Eucharistic Prayer IV: "He (Christ) sent the Holy Spirit from you, Father, as *his first gift to those who believe,* to complete his work on earth and bring us the fullness of grace."

The Holy Spirit is the Gift of the Father and the Son.[5]

The gifts of the Spirit

In writing to the Church at Corinth, St Paul treats of the spiritual gifts *(charismata)* which were so much in evidence in that community. Their very profusion posed a problem and the apostle was at pains to regulate their use. His advice is as relevant today as in those early times.

He makes it clear that these gifts are not to be sought for their own sake. They are given in view of a service to the community. They are to be received with gratitude and ministered with care and respect for others. Their purpose is to build up and consolidate the Christian community, not to place the recipient of these gifts on a pedestal.

These gifts took many forms. Some were rather spectacular in nature, notably the "gift of tongues" *(glossolalia)*. St Paul neither dismisses or underrates any of these gifts. Used wisely they serve to build up the Body of Christ. But they can be abused, as was the case in Corinth where pride and self-assertion were undermining the unity of the Church.

St Paul lays down rules for the regulation of these gifts. He then goes on to speak of the least spectacular and most important of all the spiritual gifts: the *charisma* of love or charity. We should read not only the short extract of 1 Corinthians given for today's Mass, but all of chapters twelve to fourteen of this letter. Above all, we should read and meditate on chapter thirteen which is made up of Paul's great "canticle of love". This is the gift which is superior to all the others: it is the one which will endure for ever.

It is for an increase of this love that we pray in the Mass of Pentecost. The entrance antiphon reminds us that "the love of God has been poured into our hearts by his Spirit living in us". The alleluia verse is a cry to the Spirit of love: "Come, Holy Spirit, fill the hearts of your faithful; and kindle in them the fire of your love, Alleluia!" And it is in the eucharist that we have access to this best of gifts: "Lord, through this eucharist, send the Holy Spirit of Pentecost into our hearts to keep us always in your love" (prayer after communion).

There is a diversity of gifts, but the Spirit who inspires them is one; and the effect of these gifts, all working harmoniously together, is to produce unity. Unity in diversity, that is what should characterise the Church. The Spirit respects the liberty, individuality and special talents of each; he distributes his gifts wherever and to whom he will, but in all his operations he is exercising that unifying influence which makes the Church on earth a reflection of the Blessed Trinity.

Pentecost is an enduring symbol of unity, just as Babel is a symbol of disunity. At Pentecost the disciples received the tongues of fire and began to speak to different races in their own languages; the building of the tower of Babel resulted in a confusion of languages, people no longer understanding one another. How well this is expressed in one of the intercessions: "At Pentecost you reversed the disaster of Babel, which divided and confused the family of man; through your Holy Spirit let all men speak the same language of faith and love" (evening prayer).

The Holy Spirit brings about unity, and where unity already exists he perfects it. As the disciples watched in prayer for the coming of the Spirit they were already united in hope and longing. They had come together "in one place"; in the Greek *(epi to auto)* there is the underlying idea that they had come together not just in one place but with "unity of purpose". They were thus disposed to receive this further gift of unity and charity which the Spirit would bestow. This is beautifully expressed in one of the antiphons of the old Latin breviary:

There came a divine fire which did not burn

but illumined, did not consume but gave light; and it found the hearts of the disciples ·clean receptacles, and bestowed on them the charismatic gifts, alleluia. The Spirit found them united in love *(concordes caritate)*, and filled them with the grace of the Godhead.[6]

The Church's mission

At the Ascension the apostles received their mandate to preach the gospel to all nations. At Pentecost they were empowered to carry out their mission. In St John's gospel, read today, Jesus makes the apostles sharers in the mission he himself has received from the Father: "As the Father sent me, so I am sending you"; and then he breathed on them and said: "Receive the Holy Spirit. . . ."

From its very beginning, from the time of its manifestation to the world on Pentecost Day, the Church has shown itself to be a missionary Church. In the words of the Vatican Council: "The Church on earth is by its very nature missionary since, according to the plan of the Father, it has its origin in the mission of the Son and the Holy Spirit."[7]

On receiving the Spirit the apostles became new men. Their fear vanished and they began there and then to preach the Good News to the multitudes gathered in Jerusalem. They proclaimed the "mighty works of God" and "that very day about three thousand were added to their number". There is a clear connection between the gift of the Spirit and the Church's mission.

It is the Holy Spirit who inspires a sense of mission in the hearts of the faithful. As with the apostle Paul, they are led by the "Spirit of Jesus". Moved by his grace, they feel impelled to share with others what they themselves have received. They become bearers of the Good News to their fellow men and women, making known to them the faith and salvation that comes from Christ.

Through the missionary work of the Church, God's plan of salvation is carried forward in the world. It is his will that everyone should be saved and reach full knowledge of the truth (cf. *1 Tm 2:5*). It is in obedience to this will of the Father that Jesus accomplished the work entrusted to him. The Church, in obedience to its Founder and aided by his Spirit, continues the saving work of Christ in the world.

The Gospel must be preached to the whole of creation, and the Church, the sacrament of salvation, must be made present to all peoples. This is the special work and vocation of the missionary orders and societies. These missionaries devote their lives to the task of evangelising the peoples of the world, preparing a way for the Lord and implanting the Church were it was not present before,

But if all are not missionaries in the technical or restricted sense, all the faithful share in the Church's missionary activity. By reason of our baptism we are called to the apostolate and so to a mission. The mission may be a hidden one, such as that exercised by St Thérèse, a mission of prayer by which she sought to "evangelise the evangelists". It is also a mission of example, showing by the kind of lives we lead the truths and values we profess.

Conclusion

With the feast of Pentecost the paschal season draws to a close. It is an end and a beginning: an end to the Easter celebrations and a new setting forward in our Christian pilgrimage. The period we now enter upon, known as Ordinary Time, is the time of the Spirit, it is a continuing Pentecost. The Acts of the Apostles began with Pentecost and the feast we have just celebrated is a new beginning for the Church and for ourselves.

Our lives must be permeated with the Spirit. In that Spirit our relationship to the Father must be that of adopted sons and daughters in Jesus Christ. Love, of God and of our neighbour, must be the guiding principle and motive-force of our existence. We must imitate God "as children of his that he loves" (Ep 5:1). Pentecost is a point of departure and a programme. What is now required of us is summed up in the little prayer which concludes the paschal season: "Almighty Father, let the love we have celebrated in this Easter season be put into practice in our daily lives."

Notes

1 The meaning of Paschaltide

1. Numbers 22 to 26 treat of Easter Time.
2. *La Pentecôte* (Desclée, Tournai, 1965), pp 52-7.

2 The joy of Paschaltide

1. From sermon 252 in *The Fathers of the Church*, vol. 38 (New York, 1959), p 332.
2. Tuesday of third week, *Divine Office* 11, pp 537-8, and Saturday of fifth week, *ib.*, pp 600-1.
3. Sermon 243, *Fathers of the Church*, vol. 38, p 278.
4. Letter 1 in the edition of *A Library of the Fathers* (Oxford, 1854), pp 12-13 in the second part of this volume.
5. See *Saints in Season*, edited by A. Flannery, OP (Dominican Publications, Dublin), p 210.

3 Scripture in Paschaltide

1. See Ph. Rouillard, "Les lectures bibliques des messes du dimancheau Temps pascal" in *Assemblées du Seigneur* 22 (Du Cerf, Paris, 1972), pp 53-4.
2. An interesting treatment of the iconography of the Good Shepherd is found in *The New Catholic Encyclopedia*.

3.   O. Kiefer, "Jésus et les siens" in *Assemblées du Seigneur* 25, p 59.

4.   Vatican II, *Constitution on the Sacred Liturgy*, art. 5.

5.   See *Jerome Bible Commentary*, p 255.

4   Paschal sacraments

1.   See my book, *Lent and Holy Week* (Veritas, Dublin, 1976), pp 27-38.

2.   Consult the article, "Catechumenate" by J.A. Jungmann, in *The New Catholic Encyclopedia*. Also, *The Church at Prayer: Introduction to the Liturgy*, edited by A.G. Martimort (Irish University Press), especially p 230 for references.

3.   The new Rite of Adult Baptism envisages a postbaptismal period of "mystagogical catechesis".

4.   Cf. *L'Enlise en Prière*, edited by A. Martimort (Desclée, Paris, 1965), p 733.

5.   Rev. Professor Balthasar Fisher, to whom I owe this information, describes this as an "iconographic rule".

6.   References and commentary in *Lent and Holy Week* (mentioned above), pp 30-6.

7.   *Constitution on the Sacred Liturgy*, article 48.

8.   These are found in Vol. II of *Divine Office* in the following order: Saturday of Easter octave (p 427f), Tuesday, Wednesday and Thursday of second week (pp 511f, 515f, 519f); Sunday and Thursday of third week (pp 503f and 543f); also Wednesday of fourth week (p 565f).

5   Ascension into glory

1.   R. Koch in his article "Ascension" in *Encyclopedia of Biblical Theology* (Sheed and Ward, 1976), pp 37-42, reference on p 39.

2. J. C. Murray, "Ascension of Jesus Christ" in *New Catholic Encyclopedia*. An excellent treatment of the theology of the Ascension.

3. *"Quia igitur Christi ascensio nostra provectio est; et quo processit gloria capitis, eo spes vocatur et corporis . . ."* (Sermon 73, first for the Ascension, *PL* 54, 394-96).

6   Presence and promise

1. From a reading in volume III of *The Divine Office*, p 164.

2. Sermon 2 on the Ascension, pp 641-43 of the breviary. For Latin text: *PL* 54, 396-400.

3. *Apol. Prophetae David* 12, 58; *PL* 14, 875.

4. Text in *The Divine Office* III, pp 45* and 46*.

7   Pentecost Sunday

1. His well-known work on the charismatic movement bears the title, *A New Pentecost* (published by Darton, Longman and Todd).

2. From his treatise *Against the Heresies*; extract in *Divine Office* II, pp 712-13.

3. See J. Dupont, "La nouvelle pentecôte" in *Assemblées du Seigneur* 30, pp 30-34; also R. Le Deaut, "Pentecost" in *Doctrine and Life* 20 (May 1970), pp 250-67.

4. Under the heading "Glorification du Christ et don de l'Esprit dans le Nouveau Testament", p 38 of his book.

5. This is the theme of a reading from a treatise of St Hilary *On the Trinity* in *The Divine Office* II, pp 690-92.

6. *"Advenit ignis divinus non comburens sed illuminans, non consumes sed lucens: et invenit corda discipulorum receptacula munda: et tribuit eis charis-*

matum dona, alleluja. Invenit eos concordes caritate,
et collustravit eos inundans gratia Deitatis."
(Thursday of Octave in the Monastic Breviary.)

Bibliography

Historical Background to Paschaltide

R. CABIÉ, *La Pentecôte – l'evolution de la Cinquaintaine au course des cinq premiers siècles*, Desclée, Tournai, 1965. The main ideas and conclusions of this work are contained in an article, "La Cinquaintaine pascale – 'grande dimanche'" in *La Maison-Dieu 83* (1965), pp 131-39.

Scriptural commentary

Scripture in Church, a periodical published by Dominican Publications, Dublin (also an American edition). For Lent and Easter Time readings, see Nos. 1, 6, 10, 18 and 22.
Assemblées du Seigneur, a series of short volumes on the readings of the liturgical year, published by Éditions du Cerf, Paris. Vols. 22 to 30 inclusive cover the entire paschal cycle.
BROWN, S., "The Good News Today: Reflections on the Passion-Paschal Lessons" in *Worship* 50 (March 1976), pp 163-72.

Liturgical commentary

FLICOTEAUX, E., *The Splendour of Pentecost* (tr. from French), Helicon Press, Baltimore, 1961. Good spiritual and liturgical commentary, but pre-dates revised liturgical books.
NOCENT, A., *Célébrer Jésus-Christ*, Vol. IV: *Triduum Pascal, Temps Pascal*, Jean-Pierre Delarge, Editions Univer-

sitaries, Paris 1976. A very comprehensive study; there is nothing comparable in English.

ASHWORTH, H., "I Temi Patristici del Tempo Pasquale nella Liturgia delle Ore" in *Rivista Liturgica 2* (March-April, 1974), pp 236-46.

COLESS, G., "Mysterium-Sacramentum: Some Paschal Texts in the *Sacramentarium Veronense*" in *American Benedictine Review* 27 (March 1976), pp 85-104.

FLANAGAN, P., "The Paschal Prefaces" in *The Furrow* (April 1976), pp 210-215.

Ascension and Pentecost

New Catholic Encyclopedia: articles on "Ascension of Jesus Christ" by J. Quinn (Biblical) and J. Murray (Theological); also article on Pentecost.

Bauer Encyclopedia of Biblical Theology, Sheed and Ward, London, 1970(76). Article "Ascension" by R. Koch.

DANIELOU, J., *The Bible and the Liturgy*, published by University of Notre Dame Press, 1956, and by Darton, Longman and Todd, 1960. Treats of *Ascension*, pp 303-18, and *Pentecost*, pp 319-32.

LE DEAUT, R., "Pentecost and Jewish Tradition" in *Doctrine and Life* 20 (May 1970), pp 250-67.

LIPINSKI, E., *et al; Fête de la Pentecôte* in series *Assemblées du Seigneur* NO. 30, Editions du Cerf, Paris, 1970.

MAHER, W., "The Pentecostal Experience in Acts" in *Doctrine and Life* 26 (May 1976), pp 307-13.

SUENENS, Cardinal, *A new Pentecost?* Darton, Longman and Todd, London, 1975.

SCHILLEBEECKX, E., "Ascension and Pentecost" in *Worship* 35 (May 1961), pp 336-63.

WANSBROUGH, H., *The Holy Spirit*, in the series *Scripture of Meditation:* 9, St Paul Publications, Slough, 1973.